The Tale of Toxic Positivity

by Beatrix Pottymouth

and Paul Magrs

HarperCollins*Publishers*

HarperCollins*Publishers*
1 London Bridge Street
London SE1 9GF

www.harpercollins.co.uk

HarperCollins*Publishers*
1st Floor, Watermarque Building,
Ringsend Road, Dublin 4, Ireland

First published by HarperCollins*Publishers* 2022

10 9 8 7 6 5 4 3 2 1

A catalogue record of this book is
available from the British Library

ISBN 978-0-00-855815-4

Printed and bound in Latvia

This book is produced from independently certified FSC™ paper
to ensure responsible forest management.

For more information visit: www.harpercollins.co.uk/green

for Jeremy

*

" Hurray
for me!"

A letter from Beatrix.

It is said that the effect of living in the countryside is "beneficial".

That is why I have decided to make a few changes.

I am going to live a better and more mindful life, away from the hurly-burly and the horrid distractions of the city.

I am going
to live in a
not-very-expensive
cottage in the hills and
I am going to let the
sounds and sensations
of our natural world
wash over me.

(oh, joy!)

I am sure they
will soothe
my tired soul.

all we have to do
is pause and breathe
deeply. We must open our
eyes and hearts and then we
will see – I believe – all the
things that have
been missing from
our
lives.

"Aaiieee!"

So I am taking my sketchbook and pencils and my tin of watercolours with me everywhere and I am going to observe the world around me.

You see, the living things

here in the wilderness might be small but I find myself obsessed with them all. I believe that all living things are possessed of their own unique charms and I have learned much already.

The animals' way
of life is so much
more in tune with the
ebb and flow of nature
than ours is.

   And so let us listen
— very carefully —
to our small
friends

← Tit

as they go about their
unspoiled, innocent, natural
lives in the heart
of the wonderful
countryside...

And if it doesn't work
out, I'll fuck off
to Monte Carlo.

love, Beatrix.

xxx

"Is this new book going to be just loads more animals saying 'fuck' and 'bugger' and 'bollocks' again ... ?"

"Some people are just so _busy_.

Running half-marathons for charity...

Learning to bake artisanal bread...

Others sing operatic arias and have thousands of fans listening to them...

And all I do is bugger about in the vegetable patch."

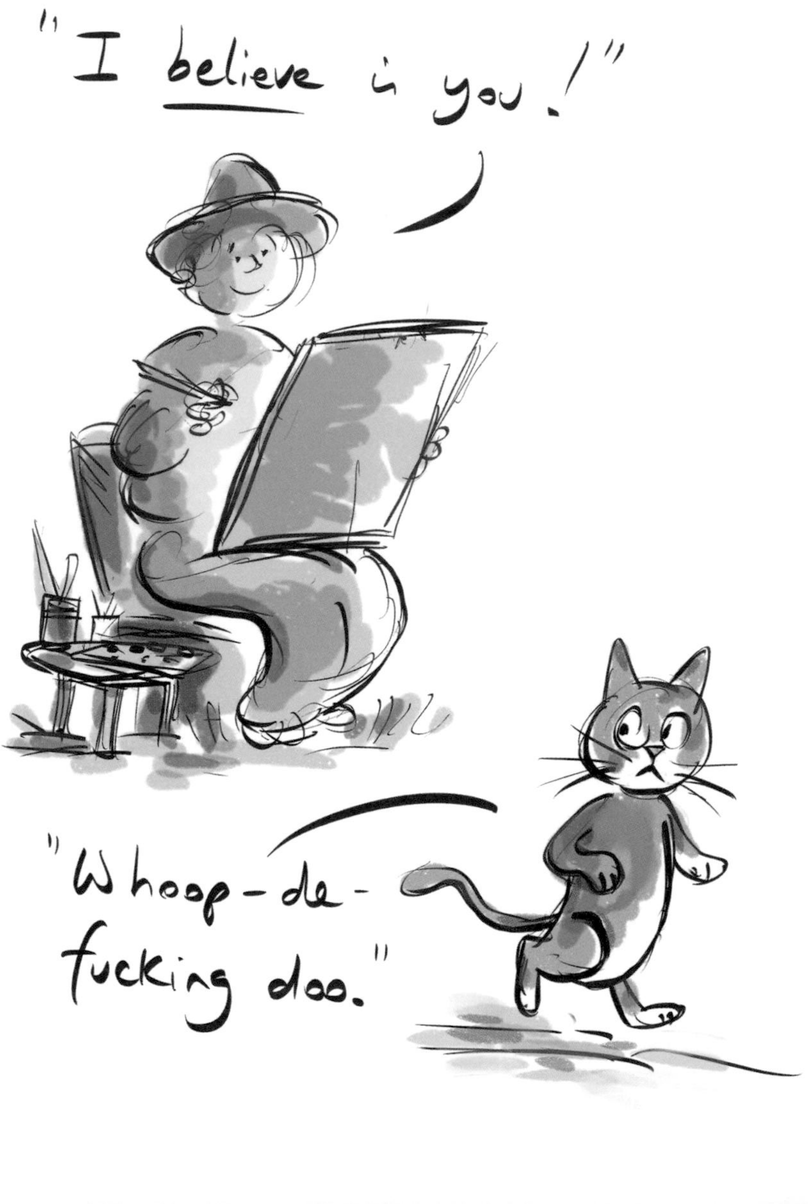
"I believe in you!"
"Whoop-de-fucking doo."

"I wish I'd put some pants on now."

"I really can't be arsed today."

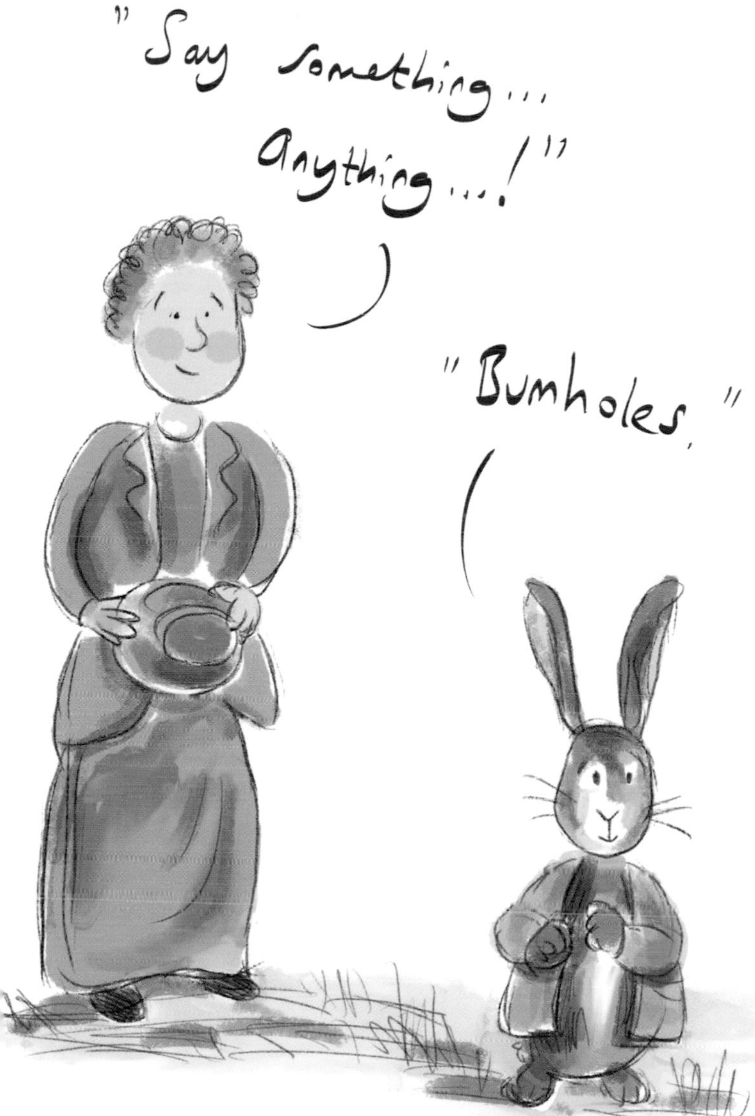
"Say something... anything...!"
"Bumholes."

"I'm not entirely sure about this business of going outside."

" Let's all think positive thoughts! "

"It's definitely wine o'clock."

"fishing is shit. I wonder if anyone's up for a shag?"

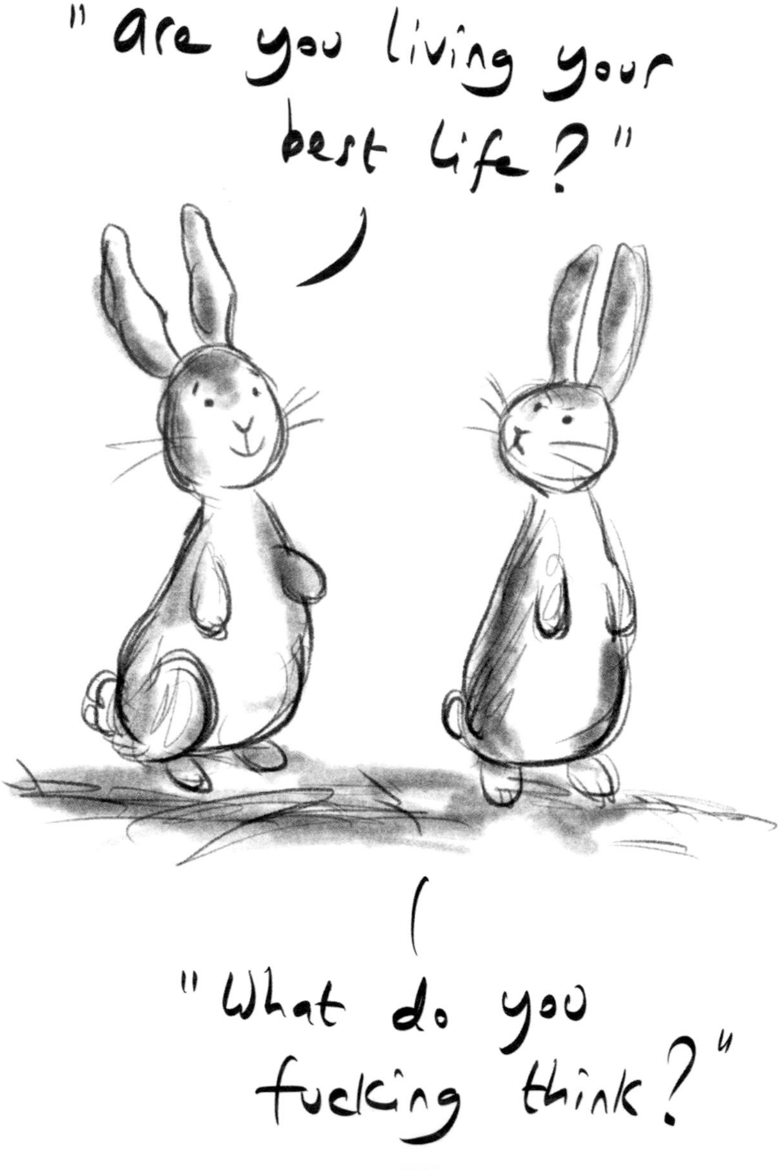
"are you living your best life?"
"What do you fucking think?"

"How lovely! We love vegan food! It's much nicer!"
"Ugh."
"Tastes like arse."

"I actually preferred it when there was social distancing."

"Our to-do list today should be all about being kind to ourselves.
Let's get pissed."

"Get a load of this outfit, motherfuckers."

"Everything is lovely.

I just wish I had bigger knockers."

"I fucking love being a squirrel!"

"I wish you'd fuck off and hibernate."

"I'm showing my fat, furry
arse to everyone
who has annoyed me recently."

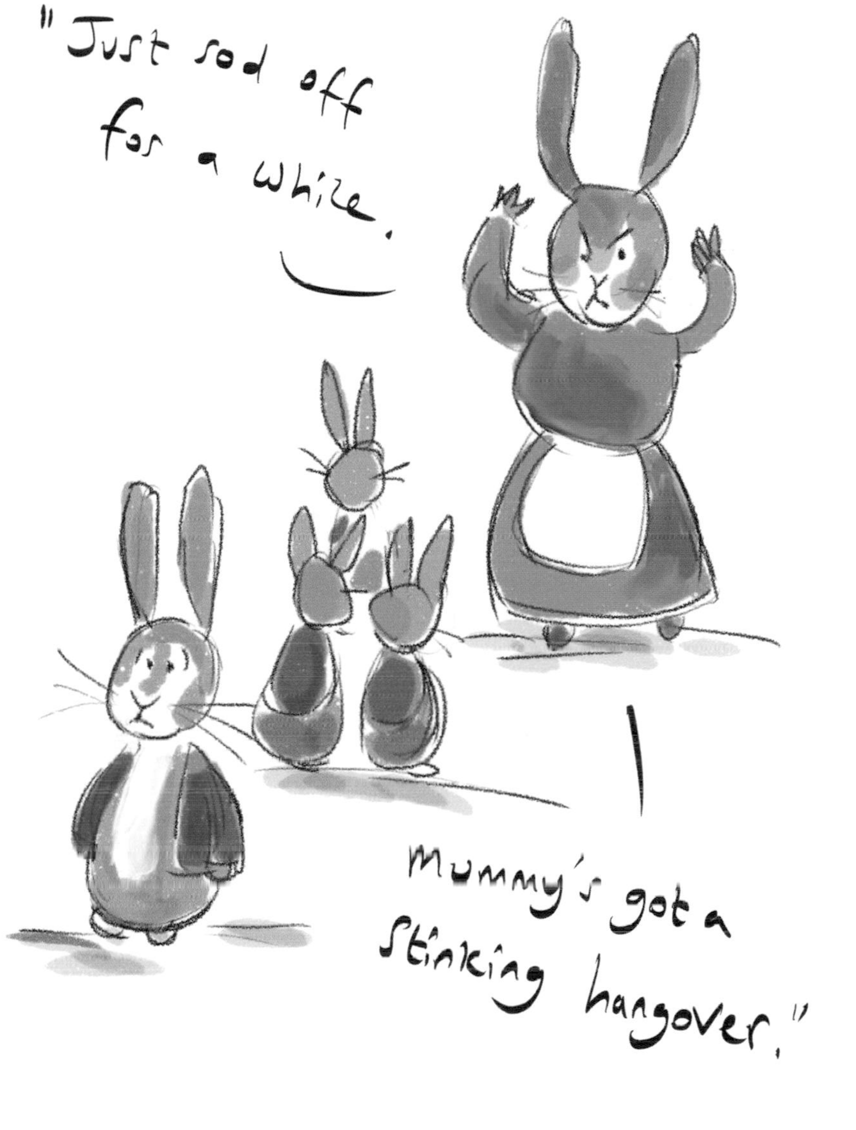
"Just sod off for a while.
Mummy's got a stinking hangover."

"I'm just so grateful for all the good things in my life!"
"She's so fucking smug."

Mrs Bunny sells herbs.
Rabbit tobacco, she calls it.

" Our mummy's always off her tits on something. "

"Ironing...?
fuck
that
shit."

"I don't judge anyone's
lifestyle
choices," said
Mr. Fox.

But he did, really.
He was a snobby
cunt.

"To be honest, I'm finding life as a duckling to be one big fucking disappointment after another."

When fuck all
fits you anymore.

"I'm so full
of empathy!"

"Oh? I thought
you were just a
big-arsed, show-off git."

" Not much bloody fun
being a rabbit."

"Why is everything so much fricking effort?

I'm worn out before I even start!"

"Seriously, mate, fuck off
or I'm calling the pigs."

"Shall we go and see if Beatrix is still awake?"
"But it's very late!"
"I can't stand her."

clink
clink

"Ho ho ho! I've got a wheely big suitcase of booze for the party! I'm gonna get fucking mortal."

"Hello, Miss Pottymouth! Can we come in? We've all brought a bottle!"

"Get some bloody tunes playing, Bea! What records have you got?"

"Oh! I'm afraid I don't go in much for dancing and loud music..."
"It's ok! I've found her ABBA tape!"

"We all love a nice dance!"

"I am the dancing queen..."

Twerk Twerk

"Ooo-oo!"

"He's off his tiny tits!"

"What's all this shit in your drinks cupboard? Where's the gin?"
"Oh dear, they're becoming rather rowdy!"

"Your rough friends are trashing my lovely home!"
"I thought you were having fun!"

"I think Beatrix would like it if we left now..."
"Never mind all that shit... Look! Prosecco...!"
"Yippee!"

"Someone's at the door! I think it's the pigs!"

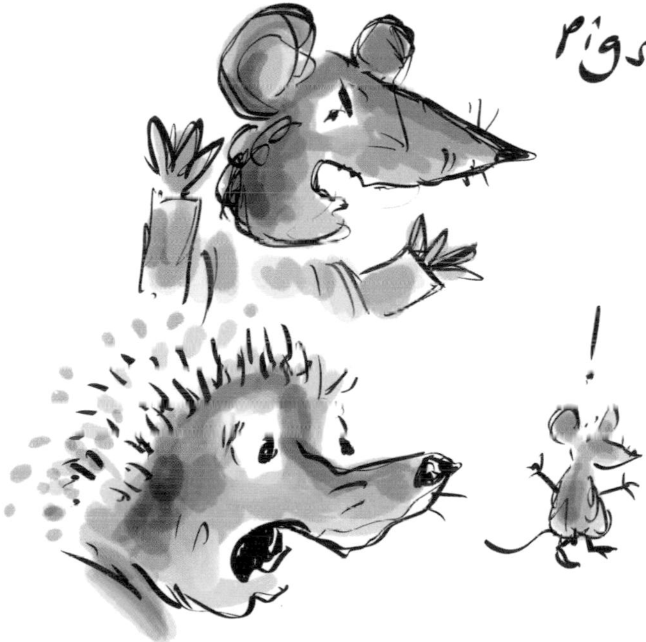

"If Old Owl hears about this, We'll get <u>Knacked</u>."

"Are we all going to get into _trouble_

just for trying to have ourselves some fecking _fun_...?"

"Oh dear! Why is Mr fox rolling about on the carpet ...?"
"He's always like this when he's had a skinful."
"aaarggh! I hate my fucking life!"

"So they all left soon after that friendly warning from the pigs,

and I vowed never to let them into my house again. They are a bunch of fucking animals."

"Own up! That was a party you threw at Beatrix's house, wasn't it?"

"It was a work event!"

"Oww, my sodding head feels like a rabbit shat in it."

"You've all got questions to answer about these naughty late-night gatherings!"

"They never happened! and we know, because we were there!"

"If we can't have any fun

What's the fucking point in any of it, Old Owl!"

"I will make a list of all the kind things I have done and then I will show it to everyone."
"Oh for fuck's sake!"

"Do you know what?
Most things you have to put
loads of effort into are a
waste of fucking time."

"Look, they're your shitty awful friends. I'd have been happy staying at home."

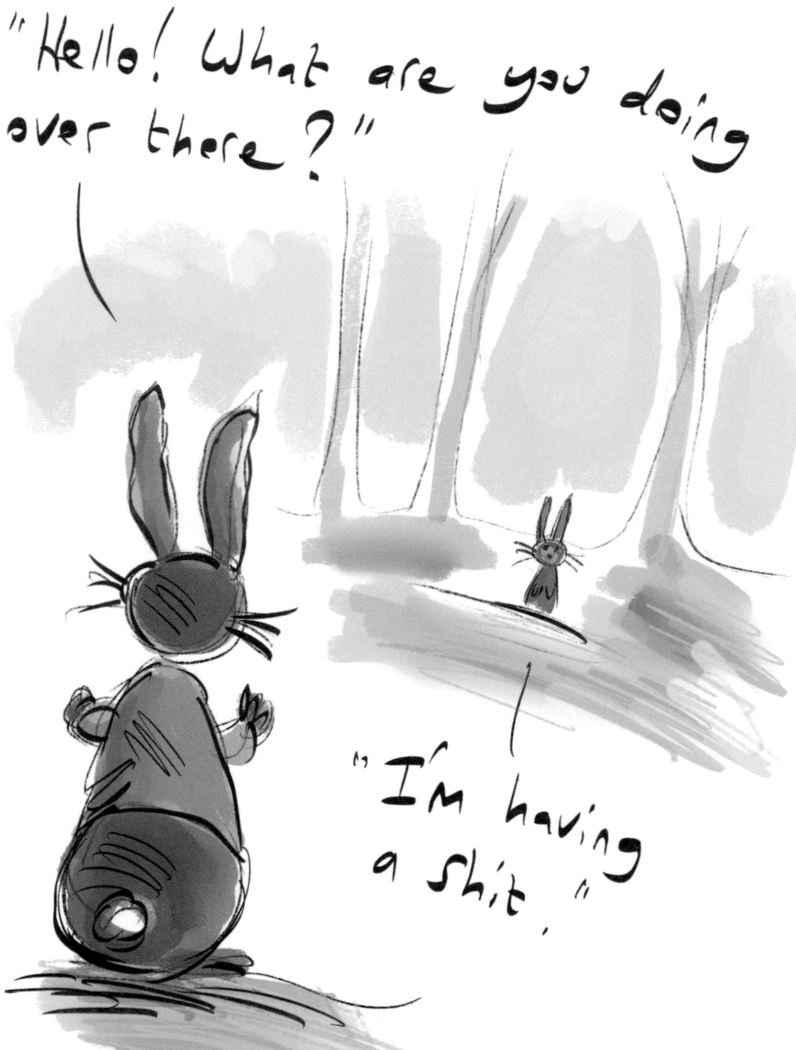
"Hello! What are you doing over there?"
"I'm having a shit."

"When you take time to live in the moment... **do** make sure it's a bloody good one!"

"Everything happens for a reason!"
"It all seems pretty fucking random to me."

"I suppose we intellectuals always tend to overthink everything."

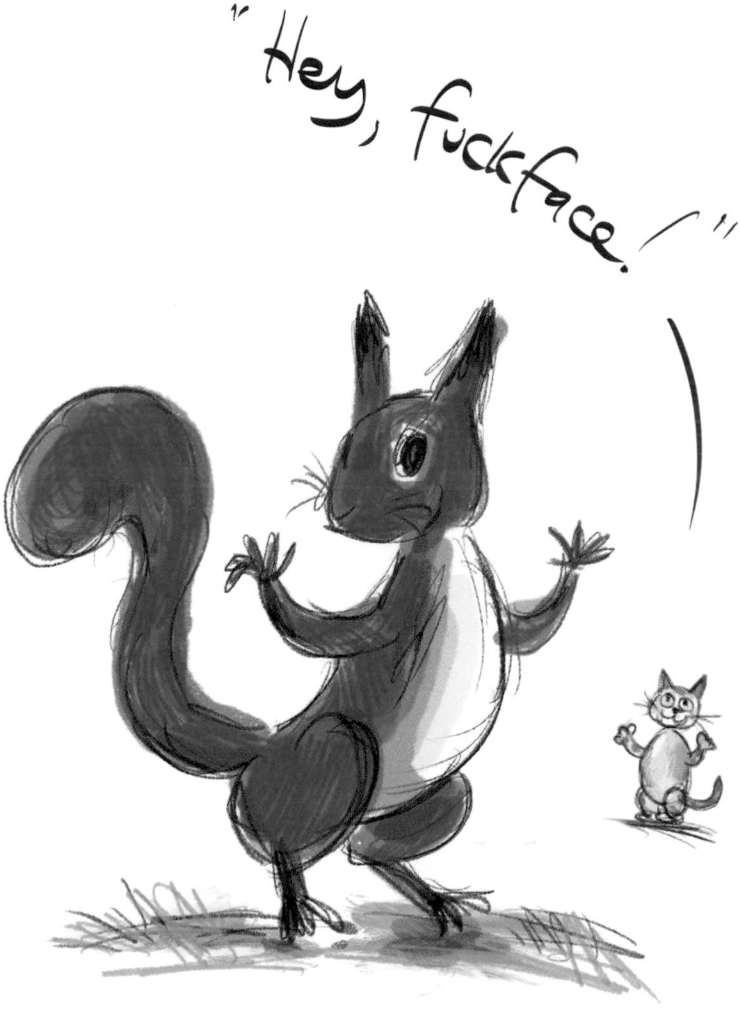
"Hey, fuckface!"

"This is what you get for swearing, you rude little bugger."

"I wonder what it's like to have boobs?"

"So basically then, all her stories are about nicking stuff and fucking shit up...?"

"Take a look at my puppies!"

"I'm the nicest, aren't I?"

"all you young wombats and bunnies are such fucking snowflakes these days."
"Yeah! fuck all you mammals. You're all so woke."

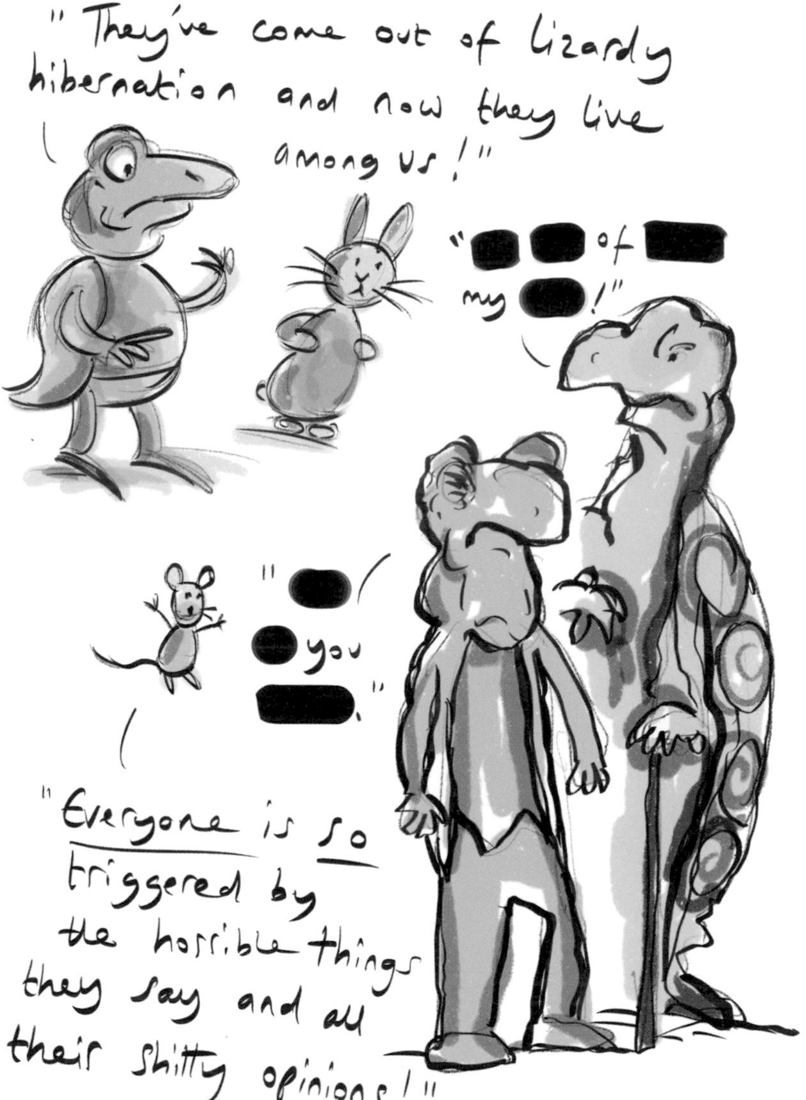

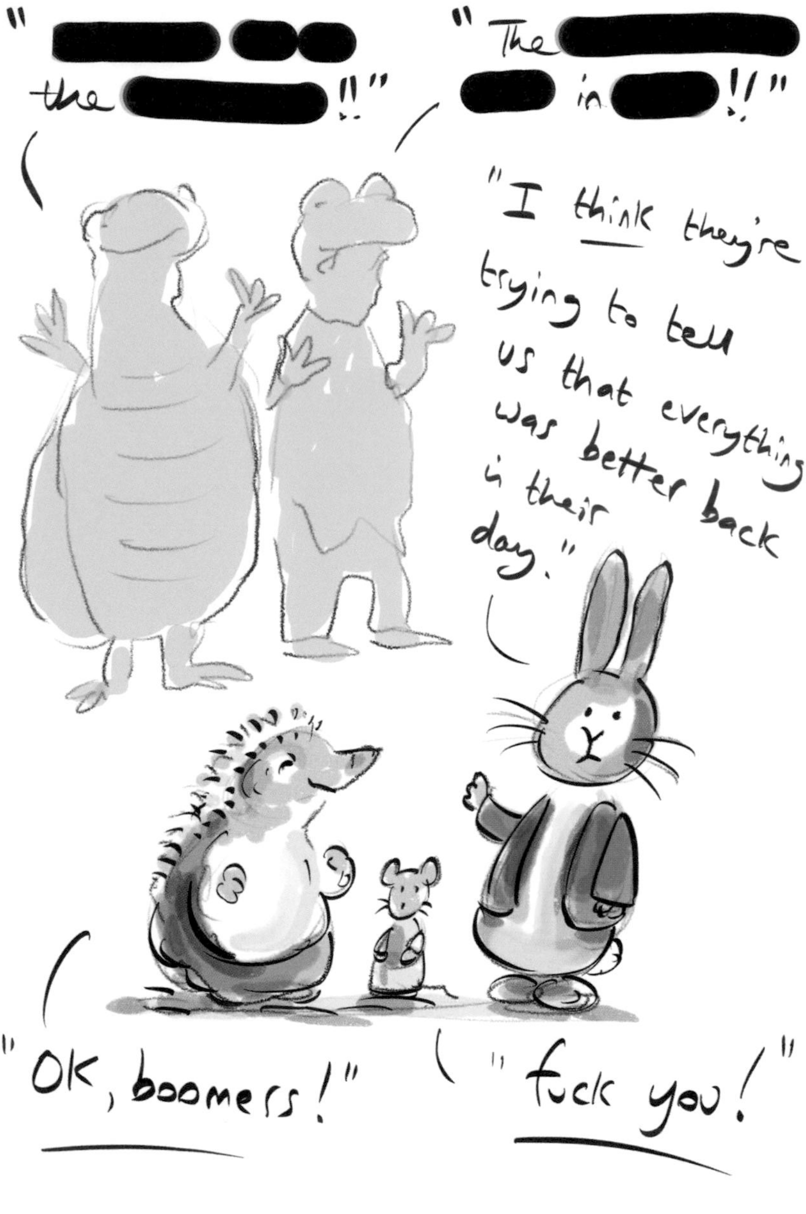

"Enjoy whatever it is you do and leave your unique mark on the world.

We'll all be dead soon."

mrs Figgy-Tinkle got caught nicking booze and ciggies from the corner shop.

— "Eeeh! I'm so ashamed!"

"Not enough hours in the day...

for all the snoozing I want to get done."

"Watch out. Mrs Bunny's having one of her sketchy days."

"Why am I always dashing about?" wondered Jeremy Fisher.

It was because he was a dopey tit head.

"Who you travel with is more important than getting there.

Unless you're with a cunt."

"Do your friends inspire you to live your very best life?

Or are they just dickheads?"

Sometimes she was so furious Mrs Bunny felt like ripping her own ears off.
"Darling...?"
"Aarrgh! I live with a fucking idiot!"

"People always say
'be yourself.'
But what if you're an awful
person?"
"Oddly enough... they're the
ones who find it easy."

That lovely
sleepy point
in the
afternoon

When it's only three
o'clock and there's lots
of reading time left.

"Does a pep talk from
your best
friend

make you feel even worse
about yourself...?"

"I make it look easy, I know. But it takes such a lot of effort."
"What does?"

"Being this _this_ fucking amazing."

"Are you easily offended
by inappropriate language?"

"Good."

"Oh dear... Why can't I be brave and tell all my friends what bloody awful people they truly are?"

"Why did I even bother having kids? Noisy little bleeders."

"I slept like shit,
so watch out."

"Am I really hearing what the animals say? Or is it the terrible promptings of my own subconscious?"

"Oh dear! are we really the sort of people who laugh at juvenile humour and rude words...?"

The fluppsy Bunnies say:
"Don't let complete wankers tell you what to think!

Read a fucking book instead!"

"Oh dear, Samuel! Why can't you be nicer and swear less?"
"Hahaha, fuck you."

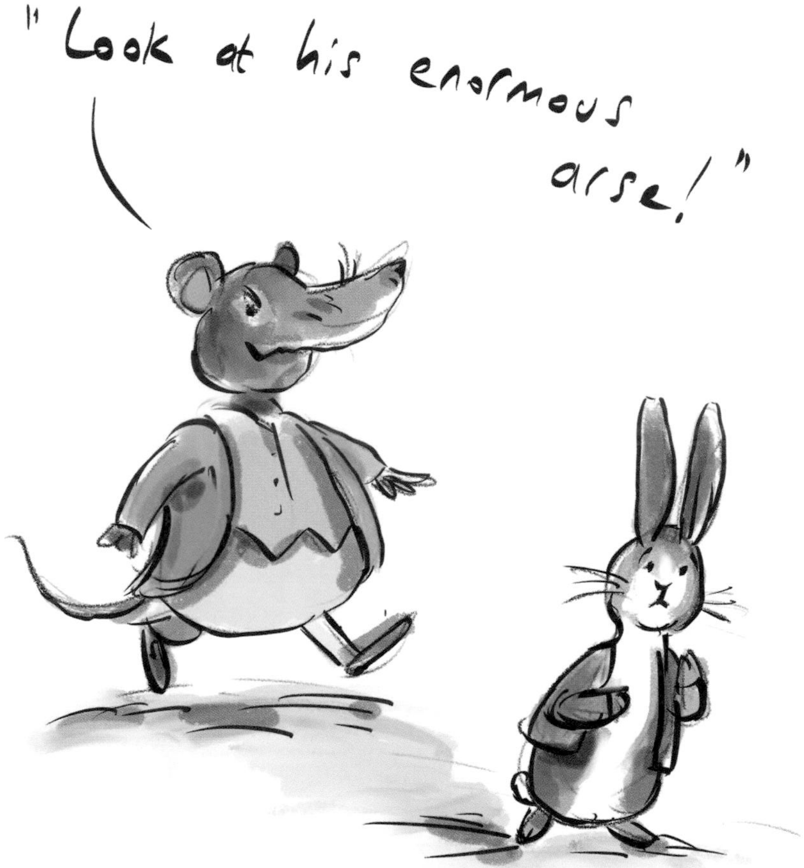
"Look at his enormous arse!"

"Quack
fucking
quack,
frankly."

"May we all find comforting mindfulness and joy and peace as we live our best lives."

"and fighting, I hope there's some fighting, too."

"Everyone I've spoken to so far today has been a complete Cock-end."

"I want to thank you for being so authentically you."
"Oh just fuck right off."

"Sometimes I think it would be lovely to be as stupid and ignorant as everyone else."

"for fuck's sake! Stop fretting and have some fun!"

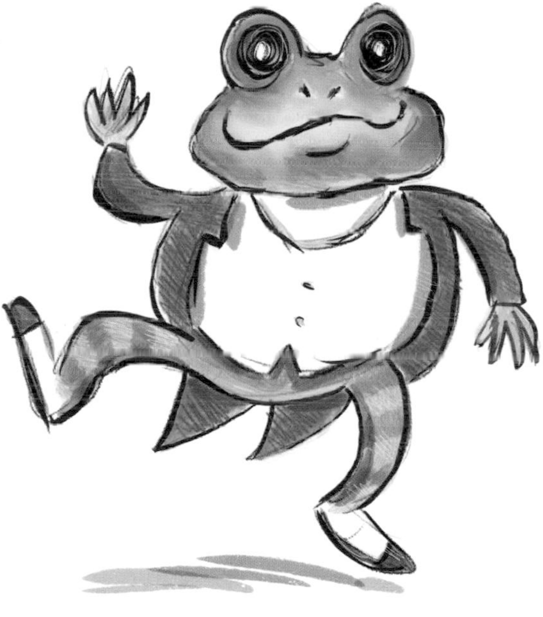

"Don't ever change, will you...?
Some people become complete
and utter arseholes."

Sometimes I feel
that I don't like
my little animal
friends at all.

They can be a
bit horrible and
common...

"Hang on...! The fucking Lake District...?
I thought we were going to Paris?!"

"Meh."

"It's a mouse in a dress!"

"Even if you're having a fucking awful day, remember to do one wonderful thing. You could read a lovely poem about nature. You could nick something from a shop. You could tell someone who really deserves it to go fuck themselves."

"'Isn't nature lovely?' they say. No! It's just all these fuckers

trying to eat each other."

"What makes you so superior?"

"Many, many things. The food chain, for one."

"Can you smell something horrible?"

"Hee hee hee!"

" I suppose you lot aren't awful company..."

In the end, what I've learned from all my little chums in the wild is that life is a _fucking_ nightmare but the alternative is _much_ worse.

"It's not quite how I planned, but I hope you find my little book about my animal chums

inspirational."

The End!

"You would probably also like 'The Panda, the Cat and the Dreadful Teddy'!"

Thank-Yous

To Jeremy and all our friends. To my agent Piers and my editor Anna and all at HC.

And thanks to everyone who's helped along the way.

Love from P‑1 ✕

Paul Magrs is a writer and illustrator who lives in Manchester with Jeremy and Bernard Socks

"and Panda."